Spending Money

BY DANA MEACHEN RAU

READING CONSULTANT: SUSAN NATIONS, M.ED., AUTHOR/LITERACY COACH/CONSULTANT

WR **WEEKLY READER**

EARLY LEARNING LIBRARY

Please visit our web site at: www.earlyliteracy.cc
For a free color catalog describing Weekly Reader® Early Learning Library's list
of high-quality books, call 1-877-445-5824 (USA) or 1-800-387-3178 (Canada).
Weekly Reader® Early Learning Library's fax: (414) 336-0164.

Library of Congress Cataloging-in-Publication Data

Rau, Dana Meachen, 1971–
    Spending money / by Dana Meachen Rau.
      p. cm. — (Money and banks)
    Includes bibliographical references and index.
    ISBN 0-8368-4872-1 (lib. bdg.)
    ISBN 0-8368-4879-9 (softcover)
    1. Money—Juvenile literature. 2. Consumption (Economics)—Juvenile literature.
  3. Finance, Personal—Juvenile literature. I. Title. II. Series.
  HG221.5.R38   2005
  339.4′7′083—dc22
                                      2005042214

This edition first published in 2006 by
Weekly Reader® Early Learning Library
A Member of the WRC Media Family of Companies
330 West Olive Street, Suite 100
Milwaukee, WI 53212 USA

Copyright © 2006 by Weekly Reader® Early Learning Library

Editor: Barbara Kiely Miller
Art direction: Tammy West
Cover design and page layout: Dave Kowalski
Picture research: Diane Laska-Swanke

Picture credits: Cover, title, pp. 4, 6, 7, 8, 9, 12, 15, 16, 17, 18, 19 Gregg Andersen; pp. 5, 11,
20 (left and lower right), 21 Diane Laska-Swanke; p. 10 Dave Kowalski/© Weekly Reader
Early Learning Library; p. 20 (upper right) Courtesy of Shirley Laska

Printed in the United States of America

1 2 3 4 5 6 7 8 9 09 08 07 06 05

T 5795

Table of Contents

You can have fun spending money at a shopping mall. Each store sells something different. You might pass a bookstore, a snack stand, or a toy horse to ride. Goods and services are names for the two types of things money can buy.

Sometimes, deciding how to spend your money can be hard.

Goods are things you can buy and take home with you. Books, toys, and games are goods. The clothes that you wear are also goods.

Apples from the grocery store are goods.

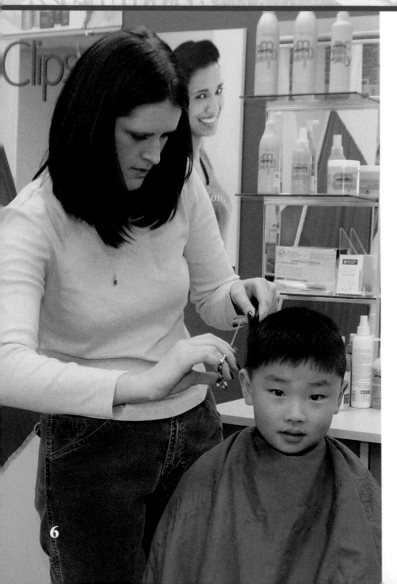

A **service** is something a person does for someone else. A haircut is a service. When a barber cuts a customer's hair, he or she is doing that person a service. The customer pays the barber for his or her work.

A haircut is a service that helps you look good.

Money travels when people spend it on goods and services. Your mother might give you a quarter. You keep it in your piggy bank for a few days. Then you might give the quarter to someone else to buy a candy bar or a new toy. Money moving from person to person is called **circulation**.

When you buy a cookie at a bake sale, the money you spend moves to someone else.

7

The government makes coins and paper money. Coins are made of metal. They can last up to thirty years. Paper money lasts only about a year and a half.

Coins are made at the United States Mint.

The government sends the money to banks. They keep the money in locked safes called **vaults**. Guards at banks keep watch to make sure the money will be there when customers need it.

Money travels to banks in **armored** trucks that keep the money safe.

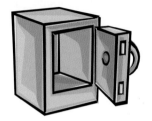

A store owner goes to the
bank to get money for the
cash register in her store.

Later that day, a man
might buy a pack of
gum from her. The
store owner gives the
man change.

On his way home, the man
might spend this change to
buy a newspaper. Money
can really get around!

Coins and paper money are called **cash**. Buying things with cash is easy, but using cash is not the only way to spend money.

Paper money and coins are made in many different amounts.

Many adults save their money in accounts at banks. They do not have to go to a bank every time they need money. They can use checks instead. Your grandmother might send you a check on your birthday.

Getting a check in the mail is a nice surprise.

A **check** is a special slip of paper. It has places for your grandmother to write your name, the date, and the amount of money she is giving you. You can take the check to the bank and trade it for cash. The bank takes the money from your grandmother's bank account.

A check must have your name written on it before you can trade it for cash.

Adults might pay for things with credit cards. A **credit card** is a small plastic card that fits in a wallet. A customer in a store can pay with a credit card instead of cash. Then he or she gets a bill in the mail to pay later.

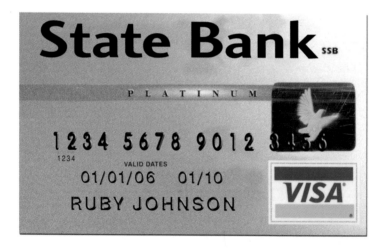

A credit card has an account number on it. The number is different for each person that has a card.

If you had ten dollars to spend at a fair, what would you spend it on? You might be hungry. You might spend all of your money on snacks. Then you would not have enough money left for a game or to go on a ride.

Would you spend your money on a big pretzel or a ride on the merry-go-round?

15

You can plan how you are going to spend your money. A spending plan is called a **budget**. A budget can help you buy the goods and services you need. It can also help you know how much money you will have left to spend on things you want.

To plan a budget, you have to think carefully about how to spend your money.

Adults need to spend money on food and clothes for their families. They pay for electricity, heat, and other things their homes need, too. They also save some of their money. Then they can plan for things they want. Going to a movie, taking a vacation, and buying a new TV are some extra things a family might spend money on.

Going on a vacation is a fun way to spend money.

You can make a budget to decide how to spend your ten dollars before going to the fair. You could plan to spend two dollars for food. You could plan one dollar for games. You could plan five dollars for rides. You could plan one dollar for a balloon.

You can use a notebook to make a spending plan, or budget.

You would have one dollar left. You could use that extra dollar for something you did not plan for. Maybe you will want another hot dog. Maybe you will want to take a second turn on a ride. You will have enough money to buy what you want when you plan ahead with a budget.

Planning helps you have enough money for the fun things you want to do.

You are going on a field trip to the zoo. You have $10.00 to spend. Look at the list of goods and services at the zoo. Plan how you will spend your money by making a budget.

Tickets

Ticket to get into the zoo
$6.00

=

Pony Ride
$2.00

=

Snacks

Soft Drinks $1.50   Popcorn $1.00

Gift Shop

Zebra pencil   25¢   Stuffed giraffe $2.50

Extras

Food to feed
the goats   50¢

Glossary

account – the money kept by a person at a bank

armored – protected by or covered with thick metal

budget – a plan for how money will be spent

cash – coins and paper money

change – the money returned when the cash used to pay for an item is more than the item costs

checks – special slips of paper that can be traded for cash by the person whose name is written on the checks or that can be used to pay for something

circulation – the movement of something, such as money, from person to person or from place to place

credit card – a small card that lets customers buy something now and pay for it later

customers – the people who pay for goods and services

goods – things you can buy and take home with you

service – something that someone does for someone else

For More Information

Books

The Allowance Workbook for Kids and their Parents.
  David McCurrach (Kids Money Press)

Follow the Money. Loreen Leedy (Holiday House)

Pigs Go to Market: Fun with Math and Shopping.
  Amy Axelrod (Aladdin)

Spending Money. Let's See, Economics (series).
  Natalie M. Rosinsky (Compass Point Books)

Web Sites

Kids and Money

www.ext.nodak.edu/extnews/pipeline/d-parent.htm
A newsletter for kids with tips on spending wisely

Kids' Money Kids' Page

www.kidsmoney.org/kids.htm
Filled with ideas and links to all money matters for kids

Index

About the Author

Dana Meachen Rau is an author, editor, and illustrator. She has written more than one hundred books for children, including nonfiction, early readers, and historical fiction. She lives with her family in Burlington, Connecticut.